W9-BRZ-521

Garfield SPILLS THE BEANS

BY JIM DAVIS

Ballantine Books • New York

SSAMINE COUNTY PUBLIC LIBRARY
600 South Main Street
Nicholasville, KY 40356

A Ballantine Books Trade Paperback Original

Copyright © 2008 by PAWS, Inc. All rights reserved.
"GARFIELD" and the GARFIELD characters are trademarks of PAWS, Inc.

Published in the United States by Ballantine Books, an imprint of The Random House Publishing Group, a division of Random House, Inc., New York.

BALLANTINE and colophon are registered trademarks of Random House, Inc.

ISBN 978-0-345-49177-0

Printed in the United States of America

www.ballantinebooks.com

9 8 7 6 5 4

MYTH MADNESS

Fed up with carrying the weight of the world on his shoulders, Fatlas breaks for donuts.

Too fat to fly, Pigasus, the winged cat, hitchhikes to Mt.Olympus.

GARFIELD®
BRRRR!
www.garfield.com
MMMMMMMM
© 2004 PAWS, INC. All Rights Reserved.
MMMMMMMMMM
JIM DAVIS 11-14
Distributed by Universal Press Syndicate

OPERATORS ARE STANDING BY TO TAKE YOUR ORDER!
www.garfield.com
Distributed by Universal Press Syndicate
I WON'T BE ORDERING ANYTHING...YOU MAY TAKE THE REST OF THE NIGHT OFF
HELLO? HELLO?
© 2004 PAWS, INC. All Rights Reserved.
JIM DAVIS 11-15

AND NOW, BACK TO OUR NATURE SPECIAL...
www.garfield.com
Distributed by Universal Press Syndicate
SHARKS WHO LOVE TOES
JIM DAVIS 11-16
© 2004 PAWS, INC. All Rights Reserved.

WE HAVE A GREAT SHOW!
www.garfield.com
Distributed by Universal Press Syndicate
AND WE KNOW YOU'LL ENJOY IT!
JIM DAVIS 11-17
© 2004 PAWS, INC. All Rights Reserved.
NOBODY TELLS ME WHAT TO DO
CLICK

WELCOME BACK TO "TELEPATHIC JOKES"!
Distributed by Universal Press Syndicate
www.garfield.com
JIM DAVIS 11-18
© 2004 PAWS, INC. All Rights Reserved.
ALREADY HEARD IT
CLICK

I LOVE HOSTING THIS SHOW
Distributed by Universal Press Syndicate
www.garfield.com
-ABSOLUTELY LOVE IT!
© 2004 PAWS, INC. All Rights Reserved.
IT MEANS I DON'T HAVE TO WATCH IT
I WISH I HOSTED IT
JIM DAVIS 11-19

OH, LANCE, THE BOMB IS ABOUT TO GO OFF!
Distributed by Universal Press Syndicate
www.garfield.com
DON'T WORRY, MARION. HERE COMES SUPER DOG TO SAVE US!
© 2004 PAWS, INC. All Rights Reserved.
JIM DAVIS 11-20
BARK! BARK! BARK!
WHERE IS HE GOING?!
SPOTTED A SQUIRREL

www.garfield.com

© 2004 PAWS, INC. All rights reserved.

Distributed by Universal Press Syndicate

NO FOOD, NO HAPPY
JIM DAVIS 11-22
GARFIELD
© 2004 PAWS, INC. All Rights Reserved.
GARFIELD
Distributed by Universal Press Syndicate www.garfield.com
GARFIELD, ARE YOU HAPPY?
GARFIELD
DINNER, GARFIELD?
NO THANKS. I JUST ATE A SMALL HOUSE
© 2004 PAWS, INC. All Rights Reserved.
COME AND GET ME, BOZO!
Distributed by Universal Press Syndicate www.garfield.com
COME ON OUT!
NO!
JIM DAVIS 11-23
THAT WAS A NUTRITIOUS MEAL!
YEAH, I DIDN'T LIKE IT EITHER
JIM DAVIS 11-24
© 2004 PAWS, INC. All Rights Reserved.
Distributed by Universal Press Syndicate www.garfield.com

JIM DAVIS 11-25
GARFIELD
Distributed by Universal Press Syndicate
www.garfield.com
GARFIELD! DINNER!
GARFIELD
© 2004 PAWS, INC. All Rights Reserved.
DISAPPOINTED?
KINDA
GARFIELD

JIM DAVIS 11-26
THERE YOU ARE!
Distributed by Universal Press Syndicate
www.garfield.com
I LOVE LASAGNA!
© 2004 PAWS, INC. All Rights Reserved.
BUT ALAS, IT WAS ONLY A FLING

GARFIELD, GARFIELD, GARFIELD
Distributed by Universal Press Syndicate
www.garfield.com
JUST LOOK AT YOU...
© 2004 PAWS, INC. All Rights Reserved.
HE'S RIGHT... I DO LOOK HUNGRY
JIM DAVIS 11-27

www.garfield.com

© 2004 PAWS, INC. All Rights Reserved.

Distributed by Universal Press Syndicate

CHRISTMAS IS COMING, AND YOU KNOW WHAT THAT MEANS...
Distributed by Universal Press Syndicate
www.garfield.com
THAT'S EXACTLY WHAT THAT MEANS
© 2004 PAWS, INC. All Rights Reserved.
JIM DAVIS 11-29

HEY, YOU!
Distributed by Universal Press Syndicate
www.garfield.com
CHRISTMAS IS COMING... GET WITH THE PROGRAM!
DECEMBER
© 2004 PAWS, INC. All Rights Reserved.
JIM DAVIS 11-30
THAT'S MORE LIKE IT

CALENDARS...THEY HURRY ALL YEAR LONG
DEC.
JIM DAVIS 12-1
www.garfield.com
-UNTIL DECEMBER...
DEC.
Distributed by Universal Press Syndicate
THEN THEY MOSEY!
DEC.
© 2004 PAWS, INC. All Rights Reserved.

www.garfield.com Distributed by Universal Press Syndicate
© 2004 PAWS, INC. All Rights Reserved.

www.garfield.com Distributed by Universal Press Syndicate
© 2004 PAWS, INC. All Rights Reserved.

www.garfield.com Distributed by Universal Press Syndicate
© 2004 PAWS, INC. All Rights Reserved.

Garfield®
PAT PAT PAT
SANTA'S WATCHING
?
JIM DAVIS 12-5
Distributed by Universal Press Syndicate
www.garfield.com
© 2004 PAWS, INC. All Rights Reserved.

HEY! NICE HAT!
THAT'S THE OL' CHRISTMAS SPIRIT!
HE MUST HAVE BEEN TALKING ABOUT MY CHRISTMAS COOKIE STORAGE DEVICE
JIM DAVIS 12-6
Distributed by Universal Press Syndicate
www.garfield.com
© 2004 PAWS, INC. All Rights Reserved.

I LOVE THIS TIME OF YEAR
COOKIES...PRESENTS... COOKIES...FAMILY... COOKIES...
MORE COOKIES...
WHO ATE ALL THE COOKIES?!
JIM DAVIS 12-7
Distributed by Universal Press Syndicate
www.garfield.com
© 2004 PAWS, INC. All Rights Reserved.

ALL RIGHT, I'LL TAKE YOU TO SEE SANTA IF YOU PROMISE TO BEHAVE
WE'RE NOT GOING
C'MON! THAT WAS MY BEST FAKE SINCERE SMILE!
JIM DAVIS 12-8
Distributed by Universal Press Syndicate
www.garfield.com
© 2004 PAWS, INC. All Rights Reserved.

Dear Santa,
I have been very good all year... And...
BOY... FICTION IS HARD
JIM DAVIS 12-9
www.garfield.com
Distributed by Universal Press Syndicate
© 2004 PAWS, INC. All Rights Reserved.

SO, GARFIELD, IS SANTA GOING TO BRING YOU LOTS OF PRESENTS THIS YEAR?
HE'D BETTER!
WE HAVE A CONTRACT AND I HAVE A GOOD LAWYER
JIM DAVIS 12-10
www.garfield.com
Distributed by Universal Press Syndicate
© 2004 PAWS, INC. All Rights Reserved.

WE RETURN NOW TO "THE LITTLEST ELF"
JIM DAVIS 12-11
www.garfield.com
Distributed by Universal Press Syndicate
© 2004 PAWS, INC. All Rights Reserved.

GARFIELD
R
WE NOW RETURN TO "LORENZO, THE SNAIL WHO SAVED CHRISTMAS"
www.garfield.com
OH, WOE ARE WE! HOW WILL WE GET THESE TOYS TO ALL THE KIDS?!
JIM DAVIS
I'LL DO IT!
LORENZO THE SNAIL!
© 2004 PAWS, INC. All Rights Reserved.
YES, 'TIS I, LORENZO THE SNAIL, HERE TO DELIVER TOYS TO ALL THE KIDS!
OUR HERO!
SO, WHAT'S THE PROGRAM? HOW LONG DO I HAVE TO DELIVER ALL THIS STUFF?
ONE NIGHT
Distributed by Universal Press Syndicate
ONE WHAT?!
LOOKS LIKE LORENZO THE SNAIL HAS OVERCOMMITTED HIMSELF
12-12

HEY, A CHRISTMAS CARD
"WISHING YOU THE VERY BEST OF THIS HOLIDAY SEASON..."
-"AND STOP CALLING ME AND ASKING ME OUT, YOU DORK. ELLEN"
WARM, SINCERE, AND IT GETS THE JOB DONE
www.garfield.com
Distributed by Universal Press Syndicate
© 2004 PAWS, INC. All Rights Reserved.
JIM DAVIS 12-13

LOOK, GARFIELD, ANOTHER CHRISTMAS CARD!
I WONDER IF IT'S FROM DOC BOY?
DOES THE POSTMARK HAVE A COW ON IT?
THE POSTMARK HAS A COW ON IT
www.garfield.com
Distributed by Universal Press Syndicate
© 2004 PAWS, INC. All Rights Reserved.
JIM DAVIS 12-14

WE NOW RETURN TO "HAROLD FENSTERNICK..."
"-THE REGULAR GUY WHO SAVED CHRISTMAS"
GEE, GUESS I OUGHTA OPEN THE FLUE...
NICE SAVE, HAROLD
© 2004 PAWS, INC. All Rights Reserved.
JIM DAVIS 12-15
www.garfield.com
Distributed by Universal Press Syndicate

A BOX!
NO, WAIT! NOT AT THIS TIME OF YEAR... IT'S NOT A BOX...
JIM DAVIS 12-16
www.garfield.com
© 2004 PAWS, INC. All Rights Reserved.
IT'S A NAKED CHRISTMAS PRESENT!
Distributed by Universal Press Syndicate

I'M WRAPPING CHRISTMAS PRESENTS NOW...
JIM DAVIS 12-17
Distributed by Universal Press Syndicate
www.garfield.com
SO DON'T COME IN HERE!
© 2004 PAWS, INC. All Rights Reserved.
-AND NO VIDEO SURVEILLANCE CAMERAS!
TOO LATE

WE NOW RETURN TO "STEWART, THE CHRISTMAS LEECH"
© 2004 PAWS, INC. All Rights Reserved.
Distributed by Universal Press Syndicate
www.garfield.com
GATHER 'ROUND, ELVES! HO! HO! H-...HUH?
JIM DAVIS 12-18
GAAHHH! GET IT OFF ME!! GET IT OFF!!!
WOW. STEW'S THIRSTY

Distributed by Universal Press Syndicate

© 2004 PAWS, INC. All Rights Reserved.

www.garfield.com

HEY, CAT
HEY, SPIDER
Distributed by Universal Press Syndicate
www.garfield.com
I HAVE A GIFT FOR YOU... LOWER AWAY, GUYS!
HAVE A LICK
OVER MY DEAD TONGUE
© 2004 PAWS, INC. All Rights Reserved.
JIM DAVIS 12-20

THE CHRISTMAS TREE SEEMS TO BE MISSING SOMETHING...
JIM DAVIS 12-21
GOT IT!
Distributed by Universal Press Syndicate
© 2004 PAWS, INC. All Rights Reserved.
www.garfield.com
IT NEEDS MORE PRESENTS!

JIM DAVIS 12-22
Distributed by Universal Press Syndicate
www.garfield.com
GARFIELD, GO BACK TO BED
I CAN'T
© 2004 PAWS, INC. All Rights Reserved.
WHO GIVES PRESENTS TO SANTA?

CHRISTMAS IS ONLY TWO DAYS AWAY!
Distributed by Universal Press Syndicate
www.garfield.com

172,800 SECONDS!

YOU LOOK PREOCCUPIED
172,797 SECONDS...
JIM DAVIS 12-23
© 2004 PAWS, INC. All Rights Reserved.

CHRISTMAS EVE...
Distributed by Universal Press Syndicate
www.garfield.com

SLEEP IS NOT AN OPTION
JIM DAVIS 12-24
© 2004 PAWS, INC. All Rights Reserved.

IT'S CHRISTMAS AGAIN, OLD FRIEND...
Distributed by Universal Press Syndicate
www.garfield.com

TIME FOR US TO EXCHANGE OUR ANNUAL CHRISTMAS GIFT...

MERRY CHRISTMAS!
JIM DAVIS
© 2004 PAWS, INC. All Rights Reserved.

To:
Garfield
THE PRESENTS HAVE ALL BEEN UNWRAPPED...
www.garfield.com
THE CAROLS HAVE ALL BEEN SUNG...
THE FOOD HAS ALL BEEN EATEN...
Distributed by Universal Press Syndicate
THE HUGS HAVE ALL BEEN GIVEN...
IT WAS ALL SO GREAT
JIM DAVIS 12-26
© 2004 PAWS, INC. All Rights Reserved.
SAME TIME NEXT YEAR?
DECEMBER

THAT WAS A GREAT CHRISTMAS, WASN'T IT?
YEAH...
www.garfield.com
Distributed by Universal Press Syndicate
REMEMBER THAT NUT LOG GRANDMA SENT US?
OH, YEAH...
© 2004 PAWS, INC. All Rights Reserved.
YOU SHOULD... YOU ATE THE WHOLE THING
I'LL BE DIGESTING THAT BABY TILL THE SPRING THAW
JIM DAVIS 12-27

HELLO, LISA? IT'S JON ARBUCKLE...
© 2004 PAWS, INC. All Rights Reserved.
Distributed by Universal Press Syndicate
www.garfield.com
-AND THERE JUST HAPPENS TO BE A HUGE HOLE IN MY SOCIAL CALENDAR FOR NEW YEAR'S EVE
JIM DAVIS 12-28
SHE TOLD ME TO TAKE MY CALENDAR AND SPACKLE IT
HOW DIPLOMATIC

DENISE, IT'S JON...
Distributed by Universal Press Syndicate
www.garfield.com
© 2004 PAWS, INC. All Rights Reserved.
HEY, HOWZABOUT JUST THE TWO OF US GOING OUT ON NEW YEAR'S EVE?
JIM DAVIS 12-29
GUESS IT'LL JUST BE THE ONE OF US
ARE YOU SURE YOU WANT TO GO OUT WITH YOU?

ELLEN, WILL YOU GO OUT WITH ME ON NEW YEAR'S EVE?
www.garfield.com
Distributed by Universal Press Syndicate
WHAT'S THAT SOUND?... SODA, YOU SAY?
JIM DAVIS 12-30
OUT YOUR NOSE, YOU SAY?
SO FAR, AND YET SO FAR
© 2004 PAWS, INC. All Rights Reserved.

NEW YEAR'S EVE...
www.garfield.com
Distributed by Universal Press Syndicate
AND HE'S ALL DRESSED UP WITH NO PLACE TO GO
© 2004 PAWS, INC. All Rights Reserved.
WHAT A PERFECTLY GOOD WASTE OF A PERFECTLY BAD SUIT
JIM DAVIS 12-31

HONNNK!!!
JIM DAVIS 1-1
©2005 PAWS, INC. All Rights Reserved.
YOU DO THAT TO ME EVERY YEAR!
BUT WHAT BETTER WAY TO START THE YEAR
www.garfield.com
Distributed by Universal Press Syndicate
-THAN WITH A CRUEL LAUGH AT YOUR EXPENSE?

©2005 PAWS, INC. All Rights Reserved.
www.garfield.com
Distributed by Universal Press Syndicate

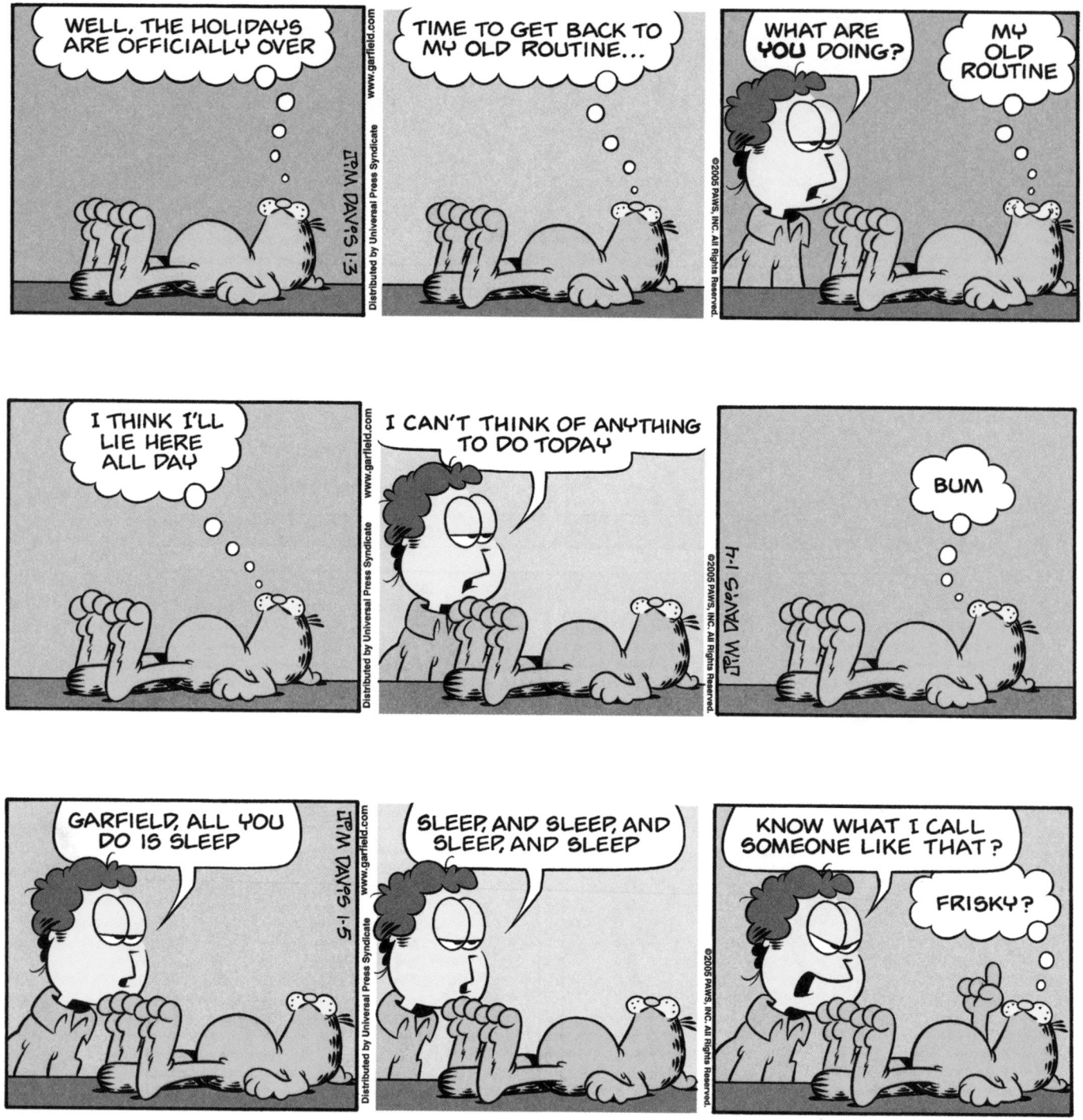
WELL, THE HOLIDAYS ARE OFFICIALLY OVER
JIM DAVIS 1-3
TIME TO GET BACK TO MY OLD ROUTINE...
Distributed by Universal Press Syndicate
www.garfield.com
WHAT ARE YOU DOING?
MY OLD ROUTINE
©2005 PAWS, INC. All Rights Reserved.
I THINK I'LL LIE HERE ALL DAY
JIM DAVIS 1-4
I CAN'T THINK OF ANYTHING TO DO TODAY
BUM
GARFIELD, ALL YOU DO IS SLEEP
JIM DAVIS 1-5
SLEEP, AND SLEEP, AND SLEEP, AND SLEEP
KNOW WHAT I CALL SOMEONE LIKE THAT?
FRISKY?

LOOKS LIKE WE'VE GOT OURSELVES A REAL DILEMMA HERE...
www.garfield.com
Distributed by Universal Press Syndicate
JIM DAVIS 1-6
©2005 PAWS, INC. All Rights Reserved.
TIME FOR A NICE NAP...
THE ICE-CREAM TRUCK IS COMING UP THE STREET!

I'D CELEBRATE, BUT THAT MIGHT COST ME MY RANKING
JIM DAVIS 1-7
©2005 PAWS, INC. All Rights Reserved.
YES!
Distributed by Universal Press Syndicate
www.garfield.com
YOU ARE THE LAZIEST CREATURE ON EARTH

I'D HAVE TO SLEEP ON MY STOMACH
JIM DAVIS 1-8
©2005 PAWS, INC. All Rights Reserved.
GRIM...
Distributed by Universal Press Syndicate
www.garfield.com
IMAGINE WHAT YOUR LIFE WOULD BE LIKE IF YOU HAD WINGS

GARFIELD
YOU MICE HAVE IT NICE
www.garfield.com
A LITTLE CHEESE AND YOU'RE HAPPY
YOU GOT THAT RIGHT
NOT SO WITH CATS
©2009 PAWS, INC. All Rights Reserved.
WE NEED MORE OUT OF LIFE
MORE?
LIKE NAPS
BUT THAT'S LESS!
JIM DAVIS 1-9
Distributed by Universal Press Syndicate
WITH CATS, LESS IS MORE

Z
HUH? WHAT HAPPENED?
YOU'RE AWAKE
OH, SO THAT'S WHAT THIS IS
Distributed by Universal Press Syndicate
www.garfield.com
©2005 PAWS, INC. All Rights Reserved.
JIM DAVIS 1-10

SOMEONE CLAWED THE COUCH
I HAVE CLAWS!
OOH! OOH! BLAME ME! BLAME ME!
Distributed by Universal Press Syndicate
www.garfield.com
©2005 PAWS, INC. All Rights Reserved.
JIM DAVIS 1-11

I CAN'T FIGURE THIS RIDDLE OUT
AND THEY PRINTED THE ANSWER UPSIDE DOWN!
OH, GREAT! THE ANSWER'S RIGHT SIDE UP, BUT NOW THE RIDDLE'S UPSIDE DOWN!
THAT'S MY EXIT CUE
Distributed by Universal Press Syndicate
www.garfield.com
©2005 PAWS, INC. All Rights Reserved.
JIM DAVIS 1-12

DOGS PUT WAY TOO MUCH EFFORT INTO DOING NOTHING
JIM DAVIS 1-13
Distributed by Universal Press Syndicate
www.garfield.com
©2005 PAWS, INC. All Rights Reserved.

ELLEN, WORDS CANNOT DESCRIBE MY FEELINGS FOR YOU...
JIM DAVIS 1-14
-SO LET ME EXPRESS THEM WITH MUSIC INSTEAD
ANNA-ONE, ANNA-TWO...
ANNA BYE-BYE, ELLEN
Distributed by Universal Press Syndicate
www.garfield.com
©2005 PAWS, INC. All Rights Reserved.

I THOUGHT WE WERE GOING TO HAVE FUN TODAY
HMMM...
REMEMBER THAT NAP WE TOOK?
MAYBE IT HAPPENED THEN
JIM DAVIS 1-15
Distributed by Universal Press Syndicate
www.garfield.com
©2005 PAWS, INC. All Rights Reserved.

Garfield®
UNNNGGGHHH
www.garfield.com
ERRRRRGGGHHHH
HUP!-AAAARRRRGGGHH
©2005 PAWS, INC. All Rights Reserved.
POP!
HA! IT'S OFF!
JIM DAVIS 1-16
Distributed by Universal Press Syndicate
♪LALALALALALALA♪
THE "PICKLE JAR LID VICTORY DANCE"

CLICK
I'M SHEDDING!
©2005 PAWS, INC. All Rights Reserved.
JIM DAVIS 1-17
I HAVE NEWS!
Distributed by Universal Press Syndicate
www.garfield.com
JON, WAKE UP!
STOP FOLLOWING ME!
©2005 PAWS, INC. All Rights Reserved.
JIM DAVIS 1-18
BEHIND YOU IS AN AWFUL LOT OF CAT HAIR
Distributed by Universal Press Syndicate
www.garfield.com
NOT ANYMORE
Distributed by Universal Press Syndicate
www.garfield.com
I BELIEVE THIS CAT HAIR IS YOURS
©2005 PAWS, INC. All Rights Reserved.
JIM DAVIS 1-19
MAY I HAVE A WORD WITH YOU?

IT'S LIKE JON ALWAYS SAYS, YOU CAN'T HAVE TOO MUCH CAT HAIR IN THE HOUSE
JIM DAVIS 1-20
©2005 PAWS, INC. All Rights Reserved.
www.garfield.com
Distributed by Universal Press Syndicate
WELL, HE DOESN'T ALWAYS SAY IT
JIM DAVIS 1-21
©2005 PAWS, INC. All Rights Reserved.
www.garfield.com
Distributed by Universal Press Syndicate
GARFIELD!
LIKE I CAN STOP SHEDDING ON COMMAND!
I'M GOING TO RAKE THE LIVING ROOM
©2005 PAWS, INC. All Rights Reserved.
www.garfield.com
Distributed by Universal Press Syndicate
I WAS SHEDDING IN THE KITCHEN, TOO!
JIM DAVIS 1-22

©2005 PAWS, INC. All Rights Reserved.
Distributed by Universal Press Syndicate
www.garfield.com

I'M BORED
OW!
YOU KICKED ME!
AND NOW YOU'RE NOT BORED!
JIM DAVIS 1-24
©2005 PAWS, INC. All Rights Reserved.
www.garfield.com
Distributed by Universal Press Syndicate

TODAY I GOT MY HEAD STUCK IN A WASTEBASKET
UH-HUH
THEN I GOT THE WASTEBASKET STUCK IN A TRASH CAN
OKAY...
THEN I GOT THE TRASH CAN STUCK IN A DUMPSTER
LET'S SKIP TO THE LANDFILL, SHALL WE?
JIM DAVIS 1-25
©2005 PAWS, INC. All Rights Reserved.
www.garfield.com
Distributed by Universal Press Syndicate

GARFIELD?
YES?
YOU GLUED MY ELBOWS TO THE TABLE AGAIN, DIDN'T YOU?
YUP
AND MY CUP, TOO!
NOW, TRY TO TAKE YOUR HAND OFF YOUR FACE
JIM DAVIS 1-26
©2005 PAWS, INC. All Rights Reserved.
www.garfield.com
Distributed by Universal Press Syndicate

TAG TEAM BEGGING
JIM DAVIS 1-27
SLAP
Distributed by Universal Press Syndicate
©2005 PAWS, INC. All Rights Reserved.
www.garfield.com

I BLAME YOU
EVERYONE ELSE THANKS ME
JIM DAVIS 1-28
Distributed by Universal Press Syndicate
©2005 PAWS, INC. All Rights Reserved.
www.garfield.com
I NEVER GET INVITED TO PARTIES

HAD A LITTLE TROUBLE WITH THE CAN OPENER
YOU'RE PATHETIC
GARFIE
JIM DAVIS 1-29
©2005 PAWS, INC. All Rights Reserved.
Distributed by Universal Press Syndicate
www.garfield.com
WHIRRRRRR...

ga
rf
ield
MY NEXT GUEST IS A GHOST
WELCOME TO THE SHOW
GLAD TO BE HERE
SO, WHAT'S NEW WITH YOU?
NOT MUCH, REALLY. I'M DEAD, YOU KNOW
AND WHAT'S THAT LIKE?
IT'S KIND OF FUN... I CAN FLOAT THROUGH WALLS, AND...
BOO!
YAAHH!
JIM DAVIS 1-30
-DO THAT
THERE WENT A PERFECTLY GOOD HAIRDO
Distributed by Universal Press Syndicate
©2005 PAWS, INC. All Rights Reserved.
www.garfield.com

LET'S TALK COINCIDENCE
IS IT ANY COINCIDENCE THAT A CANARY FITS PERFECTLY ON A HOT DOG BUN?
I THINK NOT
COME BACK HERE!
JIM DAVIS 1-31
HEY! YOU'RE THE CAT WHO ATE MY BROTHER!
YOU'RE THE CAT WHO ATE MY TWO BROTHERS!
I LOVE THIS FAMILY!
COUGH! HACK! COUGH!
JIM DAVIS 2-2
HACK
WHOA! DID YOU EVER HAVE A CANARY GO DOWN THE WRONG PIPE?
YOU'RE DISGUSTING
www.garfield.com
©2005 PAWS, INC. All Rights Reserved.
Distributed by Universal Press Syndicate

THIS DECOY ISN'T WORKING
JIM DAVIS 2-3
Distributed by Universal Press Syndicate
©2005 PAWS, INC. All Rights Reserved.
www.garfield.com

YOU MUST THINK BIRDS AREN'T VERY OBSERVANT
ON AVERAGE, TWO OUT OF THREE OF THEM AREN'T
JIM DAVIS 2-4
Distributed by Universal Press Syndicate
©2005 PAWS, INC. All Rights Reserved.
www.garfield.com

I AM A SONGBIRD
I BRING JOY TO ALL WHO HEAR ME
AND TO SOME WHO DON'T
JIM DAVIS 2-5
Distributed by Universal Press Syndicate
©2005 PAWS, INC. All Rights Reserved.
www.garfield.com

GARFIELD®
PACK PACK PACK
ROLL ROLL
ROLL ROLL ROLL
ROLL ROLL ROLL
ROLL ROLL ROLL ROLL
JIM DAVIS 2-6
UH...
BREAK OUT THE PAPER CONES AND THE STRAWBERRY SYRUP!
www.garfield.com
Distributed by Universal Press Syndicate
©2005 PAWS, INC. All Rights Reserved.

©2005 PAWS, INC. All Rights Reserved.
www.garfield.com
Distributed by Universal Press Syndicate

©2005 PAWS, INC. All Rights Reserved.
www.garfield.com
Distributed by Universal Press Syndicate

©2005 PAWS, INC. All Rights Reserved.
www.garfield.com
Distributed by Universal Press Syndicate

SNAP SNAP
YES?
SCRATCH MY NOSE
JIM DAVIS 2-10
www.garfield.com
©2005 PAWS, INC. All Rights Reserved.
Distributed by Universal Press Syndicate

MARY ONLY DATES COMPASSIONATE GUYS
I HAVE TO DO SOMETHING KIND...
I COULD GIVE SOMEONE A PEDICURE!
STEP AWAY FROM THE CAT
JIM DAVIS 2-11
www.garfield.com
©2005 PAWS, INC. All Rights Reserved.
Distributed by Universal Press Syndicate

RAIN
STOP BANGING YOUR HEAD AGAINST THE WALL!
THUMP! THUMP! THUMP!
JIM DAVIS 2-12
©2005 PAWS, INC. All Rights Reserved.
www.garfield.com
Distributed by Universal Press Syndicate

©2005 PAWS, INC. All Rights Reserved.

Distributed by Universal Press Syndicate

www.garfield.com

I HOPE YOU DON'T MIND ME SAYING...
©2005 PAWS, INC. All Rights Reserved.
www.garfield.com

BUT I THINK YOU'RE SWELL
Distributed by Universal Press Syndicate

AW, SHUCKS
NOW WHAT?
JIM DAVIS 2-14

©2005 PAWS, INC. All Rights Reserved.
www.garfield.com

Distributed by Universal Press Syndicate

I LOVE YA, BUDDY!
ME, I'M JUST BEING A PHONY!
JIM DAVIS 2-15

NOBODY IS NICER THAN I AM!
©2005 PAWS, INC. All Rights Reserved.
www.garfield.com

OH, ONCE THERE WAS SOMEONE...
Distributed by Universal Press Syndicate

...BUT I TOOK CARE OF THAT
JIM DAVIS 2-16

HUZZAH
JIM DAVIS 2-17
Distributed by Universal Press Syndicate
I'M BETTER THAN YOU!
©2005 PAWS, INC. All Rights Reserved.
www.garfield.com

YES, WE ARE
JIM DAVIS 2-18
Distributed by Universal Press Syndicate
YOU'RE AWFULLY IMPRESSED WITH YOURSELF, AREN'T YOU?
©2005 PAWS, INC. All Rights Reserved.
www.garfield.com

WHO CAN BLAME YOU?
JIM DAVIS 2-19
Distributed by Universal Press Syndicate
I'M STARING AT YOU!
©2005 PAWS, INC. All Rights Reserved.
www.garfield.com

GARFIELD®
OUT OF MY WAY, BOZO
I SAID STEP ASIDE, CLYDE!
VERY WELL. I'LL JUST STAND HERE UNTIL YOU MOVE
GARFIELD! IT'S BEEN DAYS! WHERE HAVE YOU BEEN?
WAITING FOR A GUY TO MELT
JIM DAVIS 2-20
©2005 PAWS, INC. All Rights Reserved.
Distributed by Universal Press Syndicate
www.garfield.com

SNIFF SNIFF
SNIFF SNIFF
©2005 PAWS, INC. All Rights Reserved.
www.garfield.com

AHHHH... THE SMELL OF BURNING GOATS
Distributed by Universal Press Syndicate

JON'S TURNED THE FURNACE ON
JIM DAVIS 2-21

JIM DAVIS 2-22
©2005 PAWS, INC. All Rights Reserved.
www.garfield.com

OKAY GUYS, THE COAST IS CLEAR!
Distributed by Universal Press Syndicate

ADVANCE SCOUT

I LOVE WINTER
©2005 PAWS, INC. All Rights Reserved.
www.garfield.com

FWUMP
JIM DAVIS 2-23
Distributed by Universal Press Syndicate

-ABOUT THIS MUCH

©2005 PAWS, INC. All Rights Reserved. www.garfield.com
Distributed by Universal Press Syndicate

©2005 PAWS, INC. All Rights Reserved. www.garfield.com
Distributed by Universal Press Syndicate

©2005 PAWS, INC. All Rights Reserved. www.garfield.com
Distributed by Universal Press Syndicate

©2005 PAWS, INC. All Rights Reserved.
Distributed by Universal Press Syndicate
www.garfield.com

OOOH! YOU MUST BE THE CAT WITH THE ROLLED-UP NEWSPAPER!
www.garfield.com
©2005 PAWS, INC. All Rights Reserved.
SMACK
Distributed by Universal Press Syndicate
I THOUGHT HE WAS ONE OF THOSE URBAN LEGENDS
JIM DAVIS 2-28

JIM DAVIS 3-1
www.garfield.com
©2005 PAWS, INC. All Rights Reserved.
Distributed by Universal Press Syndicate
Z
HAMMOCK

www.garfield.com
©2005 PAWS, INC. All Rights Reserved.
Distributed by Universal Press Syndicate
I HATE HUMIDITY
NO KIDDING
JIM DAVIS 3-2

IS THAT A CHAIN?
I'VE PUT ON A LITTLE WEIGHT, OKAY?!
JIM DAVIS 3-3
Distributed by Universal Press Syndicate
©2005 PAWS, INC. All Rights Reserved.
www.garfield.com

I MIGHT HAVE BEEN MORE IMPRESSED IF I WERE A SPIDER AS WELL
GOOD POINT
JIM DAVIS 3-4
Distributed by Universal Press Syndicate
SMACK!
©2005 PAWS, INC. All Rights Reserved.
www.garfield.com
ALL HAIL! I AM KING OF THE SPIDERS!

GEE, I WONDER WHAT MOM'S UP TO?
JIM DAVIS 3-5
Distributed by Universal Press Syndicate
SMACK!
©2005 PAWS, INC. All Rights Reserved.
www.garfield.com
WOULDN'T YOU LIKE TO BE LIKE YOUR OLD MAN WHEN YOU GROW UP, SON?

GARFIELD
I'VE GAINED WEIGHT
NOW I'VE LOST IT...
NOW I'VE GAINED IT AGAIN!
AND I LOST IT AGAIN!
NOW IT'S BACK!!!
YAAAAHHH!
THAT'S FOR NOT CHANGING MY BATTERIES, LARDO!
JIM DAVIS 3-6
©2005 PAWS, INC. All Rights Reserved.
Distributed by Universal Press Syndicate
www.garfield.com

WHY ARE YOU LOOKING AT ME LIKE THAT?
THIS IS THE STARE OF AGREEMENT
Distributed by Universal Press Syndicate
JIM DAVIS 3-7
www.garfield.com
YOU THINK I'M PRETTY STUPID, DON'T YOU?
©2005 PAWS, INC. All Rights Reserved.

I GUESS THAT SOUNDS BETTER THAN "GOTTA FALL DOWN"
Distributed by Universal Press Syndicate
JIM DAVIS 3-8
WAAHH
CRASH
www.garfield.com
GOTTA DANCE!
©2005 PAWS, INC. All Rights Reserved.

BAD EAR DAY
Distributed by Universal Press Syndicate
JIM DAVIS 3-9
www.garfield.com
©2005 PAWS, INC. All Rights Reserved.

TAP
TAP
TAP
TAP
©2005 PAWS, INC. All Rights Reserved.
www.garfield.com

YAAAHHH!!!
I CAN'T STAND THE BOREDOM!
Distributed by Universal Press Syndicate

IT SEEMS FOND OF YOU!
JIM DAVIS 3-10

HELLO
Distributed by Universal Press Syndicate
www.garfield.com

YAAAAHHH!
JIM DAVIS 3-11

ALL I SAID WAS, "HELLO"
YAAAAHHH!
©2005 PAWS, INC. All Rights Reserved.

Distributed by Universal Press Syndicate
www.garfield.com

YOU HAVE TUNA ON YOUR BREATH

OH, YEAH
GULP
JIM DAVIS 3-12
©2005 PAWS, INC. All Rights Reserved.

GARFIE!
BOINK
BOINK
BOINK
BOINK
BONK
SPLAT!
JIM DAVIS 3-13
HEH HEH HEH
Distributed by Universal Press Syndicate
©2005 PAWS, INC. All Rights Reserved.
www.garfield.com

SNAILS ARE SLOW
YOU
©2005 PAWS, INC. All Rights Reserved.
www.garfield.com
TAKE
Distributed by Universal Press Syndicate
JIM DAVIS 3-14
THAT BACK

DO YOU SNAILS EVER LEAVE YOUR SHELLS?
FOR ONLY TWO REASONS...
©2005 PAWS, INC. All Rights Reserved.
www.garfield.com
AND WHAT ARE THEY?
Distributed by Universal Press Syndicate
JIM DAVIS 3-15
FIRE DRILLS AND SKINNY-DIPPING

I GUESS I'LL PARK IT HERE FOR TONIGHT
JIM DAVIS 3-16
©2005 PAWS, INC. All Rights Reserved.
www.garfield.com
WOULD YOU MIND HOOKING ME UP?
NOT AT ALL
Distributed by Universal Press Syndicate
AIR CONDITIONING

SAY, YOU'RE FASTER THAN YOU LOOK
BACK AT YOU
JIM DAVIS 3-17
Distributed by Universal Press Syndicate

IT'S BEEN NICE VISITING WITH YOU, MR. SNAIL, BUT I HAVE TO LEAVE
ME TOO
©2005 PAWS, INC. All Rights Reserved.
www.garfield.com

I SHOULD BE SO LUCKY
JIM DAVIS 3-18
Distributed by Universal Press Syndicate

THEY CAN RETREAT INTO THEIR SHELLS, SHUT OUT THE WORLD, AND SLEEP AWAY

BOY, SNAILS HAVE IT GOOD
©2005 PAWS, INC. All Rights Reserved.
www.garfield.com

NAP AHOY!
JIM DAVIS 3-19
Distributed by Universal Press Syndicate

!

©2005 PAWS, INC. All Rights Reserved.
www.garfield.com

©2005 PAWS, INC. All Rights Reserved.
Distributed by Universal Press Syndicate
www.garfield.com

HEY! WHERE DID MY LUNCH GO?!
GARFIELD
Distributed by Universal Press Syndicate
www.garfield.com
BURP
GARFIELD
OH, YEAH
GARFIELD
JIM DAVIS 3-21
©2005 PAWS, INC. All Rights Reserved.

UH-OH. LUNCH DOESN'T AGREE WITH BREAKFAST
Distributed by Universal Press Syndicate
www.garfield.com
THEY'RE BATTLING IT OUT...
BURP
-AND LUNCH WINS!
JIM DAVIS 3-22
©2005 PAWS, INC. All Rights Reserved.

I FINISHED GNAWING THE FURNITURE. NOW I'M OFF TO EAT SOME CHEESE AND THEN TO CHEW ON SOCKS
Distributed by Universal Press Syndicate
www.garfield.com
GARFIELD...
I'M ON IT, JON
PACE YOURSELF!
JIM DAVIS 3-23
©2005 PAWS, INC. All Rights Reserved.

BARK
WHAT?
JIM DAVIS 3-24
©2005 PAWS, INC. All Rights Reserved.
BARK
WHAT?
www.garfield.com
Distributed by Universal Press Syndicate
BARK!
WELL, THERE'S NO NEED TO YELL

ELLEN, IF YOU HANG UP ON ME, YOU'LL BREAK MY HEART
Distributed by Universal Press Syndicate
www.garfield.com
CLICK
JIM DAVIS 3-25
©2005 PAWS, INC. All Rights Reserved.
NOWWW WE WAIT FOR THE GUILT TO SET IN
AND WAIT... AND WAIT... AND WAIT...

Distributed by Universal Press Syndicate
www.garfield.com
I ALWAYS FIND IT AMAZING HOW CATS CAN STARE OUT INTO SPACE FOR HOURS ON END
©2005 PAWS, INC. All Rights Reserved.
JIM DAVIS 3-26
Z

A LONE DONUT!
www.garfield.com
I'M WAITING FOR THE REST OF THE HERD TO RETURN
AREN'T YOU GOING TO EAT THAT?
NOT YET
Distributed by Universal Press Syndicate
©2005 PAWS, INC. All Rights Reserved.

Distributed by Universal Press Syndicate www.garfield.com

©2005 PAWS, INC. All Rights Reserved.

Distributed by Universal Press Syndicate www.garfield.com

©2005 PAWS, INC. All Rights Reserved.

Distributed by Universal Press Syndicate www.garfield.com

©2005 PAWS, INC. All Rights Reserved.

YOU CAN'T ALWAYS GET WHAT YOU WANT
I CAN, BUT YOU CAN'T
JIM DAVIS 3-31
©2005 PAWS, INC. All Rights Reserved.
Distributed by Universal Press Syndicate
www.garfield.com

IT'S HERE!
JIM DAVIS 4-1
BURP
PIZZA
YOU SOMEHOW MANAGED TO EAT THE PIZZA BEFORE IT ARRIVED
I HAVE FRIENDS HIGH UP IN THE DELIVERY BUSINESS
©2005 PAWS, INC. All Rights Reserved.
Distributed by Universal Press Syndicate
www.garfield.com

CAT TREAT!
JIM DAVIS 4-2
WHAT THIS PLACE LACKS IN AMBIENCE, IT MAKES UP FOR IN SERVICE
©2005 PAWS, INC. All Rights Reserved.
Distributed by Universal Press Syndicate
www.garfield.com

GARFIELD®
YOU KNOW, GARFIELD, I ONCE CONSIDERED BECOMING AN ACTOR
DO TELL
www.garfield.com
POSSIBLY RECITING SHAKESPEARE ON STAGE
WHOA
OR MAYBE A LEADING MAN IN THE MOVIES
REALLY?
©2005 PAWS, INC. All Rights Reserved.
I MIGHT HAVE HAD MOBS OF SCREAMING FANS
YOU KNOW IT!
EVEN MY OWN STAR ON THE HOLLYWOOD WALK OF FAME
I LIKE THE SOUND OF THIS
Distributed by Universal Press Syndicate
YES, IT'S VIDEO AND PIZZA NIGHT!
YOU GO, GUY!
JIM DAVIS 4-3

LISTEN TO THIS OLD SUPERSTITION, GARFIELD...
JIM DAVIS 4-4
www.garfield.com
©2005 PAWS, INC. All Rights Reserved.
"IF A CAT SNEEZES NEAR A BRIDE, IT MEANS SHE WILL HAVE GOOD LUCK IN HER LIFE"
Distributed by Universal Press Syndicate
SURE, LIKE THAT'S GOING TO HAPPEN IN THIS HOUSE...
WHAT

"A STRANGE DOG FOLLOWING YOU IS GOOD LUCK"
JIM DAVIS 4-5
www.garfield.com
©2005 PAWS, INC. All Rights Reserved.
"A HOWLING DOG IS A SIGN OF BAD LUCK"
Distributed by Universal Press Syndicate
AAARRROOOO
AR, AR, AR...

"IF A CAT SNEEZES, IT IS A SIGN OF RAIN"
JIM DAVIS 4-6
www.garfield.com
©2005 PAWS, INC. All Rights Reserved.
'CHOO
Distributed by Universal Press Syndicate
COOL!

KAFF KAFF
SNIFF SNIFF
I GET NO RESPECT AROUND HERE
Distributed by Universal Press Syndicate

"WASH THE PATIENT, AND THROW THE WATER ON THE CAT"
©2005 PAWS, INC. All Rights Reserved.
www.garfield.com

"TO CURE ILLNESS IN A FAMILY..."
JIM DAVIS 4-7

I LOVE THIS STORY
IT GIVES HIM HOPE
Distributed by Universal Press Syndicate

"AND HE TURNED INTO A HANDSOME PRINCE"
©2005 PAWS, INC. All Rights Reserved.
www.garfield.com

"SO THE PRINCESS KISSED THE FROG..."
JIM DAVIS 4-8

IF YOU SNEAK UP QUIET ENOUGH, NONE OF THEM CAN
©2005 PAWS, INC. All Rights Reserved.
JIM DAVIS 4-9

CERTAIN KINDS OF BIRDS CAN'T FLY

HERE'S AN INTERESTING FACTOID, GARFIELD
Distributed by Universal Press Syndicate
www.garfield.com

GARFIELD®
SNACKIE TIME
©2005 PAWS, INC. All Rights Reserved.
LET'S SEE...APPLESAUCE?... POLISH SAUSAGE?...CHEESE BALL?
CORN DOG? YOGURT? COLD PIZZA? PICKLE CHIPS?
Distributed by Universal Press Syndicate
BEEF LOG? PORK CHOP? GREEN GRAPES? PIG'S KNUCKLES? SPANISH OLIVES? WALLEYED PIKE? HEADCHEESE? POT PIE? BEAN BURRITO?
JIM DAVIS 4-10
AW, WHAT THE HECK...
www.garfield.com
I'LL JUST GO WITH THE BUFFET
UH, GARFIELD...

WAKE UP, GARFIELD! IT'S 4 A.M.!
I HAVE A GREAT IDEA!
LET'S WATCH THE SUNRISE!
OKAY, YOU CAN WATCH IT FROM THE AMBULANCE
JIM DAVIS 4-11
www.garfield.com
©2005 PAWS, INC. All Rights Reserved.
Distributed by Universal Press Syndicate

JIM DAVIS 4-12
PUSH
CRASH!
WHY DO YOU DO THAT?
I DIDN'T SEE YOU VOLUNTEERING
www.garfield.com
©2005 PAWS, INC. All Rights Reserved.
Distributed by Universal Press Syndicate

MY LIFE IS MISSING SOMETHING
THAT'S IT!
LUNCH!
JIM DAVIS 4-13
www.garfield.com
©2005 PAWS, INC. All Rights Reserved.
Distributed by Universal Press Syndicate

NAPS TAKE YOU
Distributed by Universal Press Syndicate

YOU DON'T TAKE NAPS...
©2005 PAWS, INC. All Rights Reserved.
www.garfield.com

YOU KNOW...
JIM DAVIS 4-14

ELLEN, VOODOO DOLLS DON'T REALLY WORK
OUCH!
Distributed by Universal Press Syndicate

DO I FEEL WHAT?... IN MY BACK?... MY LEG?... MY HEAD?
©2005 PAWS, INC. All Rights Reserved.
www.garfield.com

HI, ELLEN, IT'S JON
JIM DAVIS 4-15

WOW, DEEPER THAN I THOUGHT!
JIM DAVIS 4-16
Distributed by Universal Press Syndicate

PIE IS GOOD

JON APPEARS DEEP IN THOUGHT
©2005 PAWS, INC. All Rights Reserved.
www.garfield.com

GARFIELD®
YES, YOU TOO CAN BE MORE POPULAR WITH WOMEN IF YOU USE BABE MAGNET BODY LOTION!
www.garfield.com
SIDE EFFECTS MAY INCLUDE EXCESSIVE BODY HAIR...
ITCHY ELBOWS, NOSE TWITCHING...
Distributed by Universal Press Syndicate
FOOT TAPPING, LEG SLAPPING... AND FLUTTERING EYELIDS
©2005 PAWS, INC. All Rights Reserved.
WHAT IDIOT WOULD BUY THAT PRODUCT?
FLUTTER FLUTTER FLUTTER
SLAP SLAP SLAP
TAP TAP TAP
JIM DAVIS 4-17

I HAD A TERRIBLE MORNING...
-AND YOU SLEPT ALL MORNING
SO THEN, WHAT HAVE WE LEARNED FROM THIS?
JIM DAVIS 4-18
©2005 PAWS, INC. All Rights Reserved.
www.garfield.com
Distributed by Universal Press Syndicate

ODIE! THAT SPOT ON THE WALL LOOKS LIKE A STEAK!
SPLAT!
SHOOM
NOW THAT SPOT ON THE WALL LOOKS LIKE ODIE
JIM DAVIS 4-19
©2005 PAWS, INC. All Rights Reserved.
www.garfield.com
Distributed by Universal Press Syndicate

YOU KNOW WHAT?
WE NEEDED A NEW TOASTER ANYWAY
YOU'RE GLOWING
JIM DAVIS 4-20
©2005 PAWS, INC. All Rights Reserved.
www.garfield.com
Distributed by Universal Press Syndicate

YOU DON'T SCARE ME
I'M NOT SUPPOSED TO
Distributed by Universal Press Syndicate
www.garfield.com
YOU'RE SUPPOSED TO SCARE ME
JIM DAVIS 4-21
©2005 PAWS, INC. All Rights Reserved.
OOPS
ROOKIE

ELLEN, HOW'S ABOUT I ZIP OVER TO YOUR PLACE AND SERENADE YOU WITH MY ACCORDION?
Distributed by Universal Press Syndicate
www.garfield.com
JIM DAVIS 4-22
©2005 PAWS, INC. All Rights Reserved.
"RESTRAINING ORDER" IS SUCH AN UGLY WORD, ELLEN
THAT'S TWO WORDS, DUMMY

Distributed by Universal Press Syndicate
www.garfield.com
CUPCAKES
JIM DAVIS 4-23
©2005 PAWS, INC. All Rights Reserved.
MADE YOU SMILE

Distributed by Universal Press Syndicate

©2005 PAWS, INC. All Rights Reserved.

www.garfield.com

NOT THAT I SPEND A LOT OF TIME LOOKING AT IT
JIM DAVIS 4-25
Distributed by Universal Press Syndicate
www.garfield.com
GARFIELD
CAT FOOD IS DISGUSTING TO LOOK AT
GARFIELD
©2005 PAWS, INC. All Rights Reserved.
THEN WE RUN OUT OF FOOD
JIM DAVIS 4-26
Distributed by Universal Press Syndicate
FOR INSTANCE, I CAN ONLY EAT SO MUCH...
YOU GOTTA KNOW YOUR LIMITS...
©2005 PAWS, INC. All Rights Reserved.
www.garfield.com
HAVE YOU CONSIDERED FEEDING ME MORE?
JIM DAVIS 4-27
Distributed by Universal Press Syndicate
I WISH I WERE MORE POPULAR
©2005 PAWS, INC. All Rights Reserved.
www.garfield.com

GOBBLE GOBBLE SNARF GULP
©2005 PAWS, INC. All Rights Reserved.
JIM DAVIS 4-28
www.garfield.com

SQUIK SQUIK

Distributed by Universal Press Syndicate

RFIELD
JIM DAVIS 4-29
www.garfield.com

Distributed by Universal Press Syndicate

WOULD YOU LIKE ME TO FILL YOUR DISH?
WITH SOMETHING OTHER THAN YOUR FACE, PLEASE
GARFIELD
©2005 PAWS, INC. All Rights Reserved.

IF YOU BEG, I'LL LET YOU LICK MY ICE CREAM CONE
JIM DAVIS 4-30
©2005 PAWS, INC. All Rights Reserved.
www.garfield.com

The cartoonist has elected not to show this panel due to its graphic nature.

YOU COULD HAVE ASKED NICELY!
WHERE'S THE FUN IN THAT?
Distributed by Universal Press Syndicate

Garfield®

©2005 PAWS, INC. All Rights Reserved.
Distributed by Universal Press Syndicate
www.garfield.com

WELL, WELL, YOU'RE FINALLY UP!
DO YOU REALIZE YOU SLEPT FOR 23 STRAIGHT HOURS?
AND I CAN DO WITHOUT THE LITTLE VICTORY DANCE!!
JIM DAVIS 5-2
©2005 PAWS, INC. All Rights Reserved.
www.garfield.com
Distributed by Universal Press Syndicate

DOGS
DOGS CAN LOOK BUSY EVEN WHEN THEY'RE DOING NOTHING
JIM DAVIS 5-3
©2005 PAWS, INC. All Rights Reserved.
www.garfield.com
Distributed by Universal Press Syndicate

YOU'D NEVER LIE TO ME, WOULD YOU?
WAH-HA-HA-HA-HA-HA-HA!!!
OF COURSE NOT
JIM DAVIS 5-4
©2005 PAWS, INC. All Rights Reserved.
www.garfield.com
Distributed by Universal Press Syndicate

©2005 PAWS, INC. All Rights Reserved.
www.garfield.com
Distributed by Universal Press Syndicate

©2005 PAWS, INC. All Rights Reserved.
www.garfield.com
Distributed by Universal Press Syndicate

©2005 PAWS, INC. All Rights Reserved.
www.garfield.com
Distributed by Universal Press Syndicate

GARFIELD
CLICK
I LOVE THIS SHOW
IT ALWAYS HAS A HAPPY ENDING
DING
SEE?
COOKIES ARE DONE!
JIM DAVIS 5-8
©2005 PAWS, INC. All Rights Reserved.
Distributed by Universal Press Syndicate
www.garfield.com

WOMEN...
JIM DAVIS 5-9
©2005 PAWS, INC. All Rights Reserved.
www.garfield.com

WHERE'S MINE?!
MOST LIKELY IN HIDING
Distributed by Universal Press Syndicate

BAD DATE, GARFIELD
©2005 PAWS, INC. All Rights Reserved.
www.garfield.com

WE WENT TO A PETTING ZOO...

AND A GOAT ATE MY PANTS
NICE TEDDY BEAR BOXERS
Distributed by Universal Press Syndicate
JIM DAVIS 5-10

BAD DATE, GARFIELD
©2005 PAWS, INC. All Rights Reserved.
www.garfield.com

WE WENT TO A FANCY FRENCH RESTARAUNT

AND I ORDERED HER A TENNIS SHOE SOUFFLÉ
PROPERLY PREPARED, THEY'RE REALLY QUITE TASTY
Distributed by Universal Press Syndicate
JIM DAVIS 5-11

BAD DATE, GARFIELD
JIM DAVIS 5-12
©2005 PAWS, INC. All Rights Reserved.
www.garfield.com
WE WENT SAILING
Distributed by Universal Press Syndicate
EVER HAD A MIZZENMAST STUCK UP YOUR-
NO, AND LET'S TALK ABOUT ANYTHING ELSE RIGHT NOW

BAD DATE, GARFIELD
GARFIELD
JIM DAVIS 5-13
©2005 PAWS, INC. All Rights Reserved.
www.garfield.com
WE WENT TO THE FAIR AND I ATE FOUR CHILI-CHEESE DOGS
GARFIELD
Distributed by Universal Press Syndicate
THEN WE RODE THE SCREAMING WEEVIL
HEY! I'M HAVING BREAKFAST HERE!
GARFIELD

BAD DATE, GARFIELD
©2005 PAWS, INC. All Rights Reserved.
www.garfield.com
SHE LEFT IN THE MIDDLE OF THE MEAL WITH THE VALET PARKING GUY
Distributed by Universal Press Syndicate
IN MY CAR
OUCH
JIM DAVIS 5-14

©2005 PAWS, INC. All Rights Reserved.
Distributed by Universal Press Syndicate
www.garfield.com

YOU KNOW...
IT'S NOT THE SIZE OF THE NAP THAT COUNTS...
-IT'S HOW MANY YOU CAN SQUEEZE INTO AN AFTERNOON
JIM DAVIS 5-16
SO MUCH FOR HOME BARBERING
I THOUGHT I DID A PRETTY GOOD JOB
JIM DAVIS 5-17
EXCUSE ME. HAVE YOU SEEN MY UNCLE DAVE?
PERHAPS
WHAT DOES HE TASTE LIKE?
JIM DAVIS 5-18
©2005 PAWS, INC. All Rights Reserved.
www.garfield.com
Distributed by Universal Press Syndicate

THE SIMPLE ACT OF SITTING IN A CHAIR...
©2005 PAWS, INC. All Rights Reserved.
www.garfield.com
...ODIE...
Distributed by Universal Press Syndicate
NOT EVEN A WHISPER OF A CLUE
JIM DAVIS 5-19

I'M A LONELY GUY, GARFIELD
©2005 PAWS, INC. All Rights Reserved.
www.garfield.com
LONELY, LONELY, LONELY, LONELY, LONELY...
Distributed by Universal Press Syndicate
-LONELY, LONELY, LONELY, LONELY, LONELY, LONELY...
JIM DAVIS 5-20

HERE'S A PET SURVEY, GARFIELD
©2005 PAWS, INC. All Rights Reserved.
www.garfield.com
"WHAT IS YOUR PET'S MOST ENDEARING FEATURE?"
Distributed by Universal Press Syndicate
HMMM...
I NEVER KILLED ANYTHING THAT WASN'T SICK
JIM DAVIS 5-21

©2005 PAWS, INC. All Rights Reserved.

Distributed by Universal Press Syndicate

www.garfield.com

HELLO? MRS. FEENY?
JIM DAVIS 5-23
©2005 PAWS, INC. All Rights Reserved.
www.garfield.com
HE DID WHAT?
Distributed by Universal Press Syndicate
WELL, THAT DOESN'T SOUND TOO BAD
AH, BUT THE DAY IS YOUNG

RIIINNG
JIM DAVIS 5-24
©2005 PAWS, INC. All Rights Reserved.
www.garfield.com
HELLO, MRS. FEENY. HOW ARE YOU?
Distributed by Universal Press Syndicate
SHE'S NOT FINE!
I KINDA FIGURED THAT

THAT WAS MRS. FEENY
JIM DAVIS 5-25
©2005 PAWS, INC. All Rights Reserved.
www.garfield.com
ALTHOUGH SHE WAS KIND OF HARD TO UNDERSTAND
Distributed by Universal Press Syndicate
I THINK SHE SAID SHE WANTED HER DENTURES BACK
SHE'LL HAVE TO ARM WRESTLE MY SOCK PUPPET FOR THEM

RIIINNG
JIM DAVIS 5-26
www.garfield.com
©2005 PAWS, INC. All Rights Reserved.

RIIINNG
Distributed by Universal Press Syndicate

RIIINNG
I'M NOT GOING TO ANSWER THAT
YOU'D BETTER. MRS. FEENY'S ON HER CELL PHONE IN THE FRONT YARD

THAT WAS MRS. FEENY
YEEEEES?
www.garfield.com
©2005 PAWS, INC. All Rights Reserved.

WHAT'S ALL THIS ABOUT HER CHIHUAHUA AND PAPIER-MÂCHÉ?
Distributed by Universal Press Syndicate

LET'S JUST SAY THE MUMMY LIVES
JIM DAVIS 5-27

SLAM!
www.garfield.com
©2005 PAWS, INC. All Rights Reserved.

Distributed by Universal Press Syndicate

NEVER FLIRT WITH A TOUCHY GROCERY CHECKER
I NOTICE SHE DOUBLE-BAGGED YOU
JIM DAVIS 5-28

www.garfield.com

Distributed by Universal Press Syndicate

©2005 PAWS, INC. All Rights Reserved.

©2005 PAWS, INC. All Rights Reserved.
www.garfield.com

Distributed by Universal Press Syndicate

©2005 PAWS, INC. All Rights Reserved.
www.garfield.com

Distributed by Universal Press Syndicate

©2005 PAWS, INC. All Rights Reserved.
www.garfield.com

Distributed by Universal Press Syndicate

SO MUCH FOR WEED WHACKING
YOU MISSED A SPOT OVER THERE
JIM DAVIS 6-2
OH, WELL...
Distributed by Universal Press Syndicate
©2005 PAWS, INC. All Rights Reserved.
www.garfield.com
THAT'S ANOTHER PIZZA DELIVERY GUY WHO'S NEVER COMING BACK!
JINGLE JINGLE
SURE HE WILL. I'VE GOT HIS CAR KEYS
PIZZA
YAAAAAHHH!
Distributed by Universal Press Syndicate
©2005 PAWS, INC. All Rights Reserved.
www.garfield.com
DING DONG
JIM DAVIS 6-3
I WONDER WHAT'S ON TV TONIGHT
ALREADY MADE THE POPCORN AND POURED THE SODAS
Distributed by Universal Press Syndicate
©2005 PAWS, INC. All Rights Reserved.
www.garfield.com
CLICK
HI, ELLEN? IT'S JON
JIM DAVIS 6-4

Garfield®
YOU KNOW...
www.garfield.com
THERE'S AN OLD ADAGE...
THAT PETS ARE PEOPLE TOO...
Distributed by Universal Press Syndicate
HEY, GARFIELD!
CHECK THIS OUT
©2005 PAWS, INC. All Rights Reserved.
I'M TURRRKEY MAN!
AND I COULDN'T BE MORE INSULTED
JIM DAVIS 6-5

CREATE A WHOLE NEW YOU IN JUST SIX WEEKS!
©2005 PAWS, INC. All Rights Reserved.
JIM DAVIS 6-6
CALL NOW! OPERATORS ARE STANDING BY!
CLICK
WHY WOULD I WANT TO CREATE A WHOLE NEW ME?
Distributed by Universal Press Syndicate
www.garfield.com
THEN I'D JUST HAVE TO SHARE...

THIS IS A TEST...
Distributed by Universal Press Syndicate
www.garfield.com
THIS IS ONLY A TEST...
©2005 PAWS, INC. All Rights Reserved.
JIM DAVIS 6-7
WHAT IS THE CAPITAL OF NORTH DAKOTA?
THIS IS A TEST!

AND NOW, WITH THE OVERTURE TO THE OPERA "CARMEN"...
Distributed by Universal Press Syndicate
www.garfield.com
WE GIVE YOU WANDA MAE THROTTLEBOTTOM...
©2005 PAWS, INC. All Rights Reserved.
JIM DAVIS 6-8
-AND HER AMAZING KNEE CYMBALS!
I HAVE GOT TO LEARN TO READ

MY FIRST GUEST TONIGHT NEEDS NO INTRODUCTION
Distributed by Universal Press Syndicate
www.garfield.com
©2005 PAWS, INC. All Rights Reserved.
JIM DAVIS 6-9

AND NOW, FOR YOUR LISTENING AND VIEWING PLEASURE...
Distributed by Universal Press Syndicate
www.garfield.com
-IDA MAE STEPSTOOL AND HER YODELING PIG!
WHOA!
©2005 PAWS, INC. All Rights Reserved.
JIM DAVIS 6-10
YODEL-ODELL-ODELL-ODELL-AYY-EEE-OOOOOH
THE PIG LOOKS BETTER IN LEDERHOSEN THAN IDA MAE DOES

DID YOU MISS ME?
YES, I DID, JON
JIM DAVIS 6-11
Distributed by Universal Press Syndicate
www.garfield.com
IN FACT...
©2005 PAWS, INC. All Rights Reserved.
I WASN'T DONE MISSING YOU. WOULD YOU MIND LEAVING AGAIN?

MYTH MADNESS

The goddess Arlena gets stood up by Garcissus, who decides it would be more fun to date himself.

Ineptune, the bumbling god of the sea, inadvertently wipes out a small village with a tidal wave of drool.

It's a party online—and YOU'RE invited!
GARFIELD.COM
News
Get the latest scoop on everyone's favorite media darling!
Fun & Games
Tons of arcade fun for everyone. Wanna play?
Comics
Read the daily comic or browse the vault for a blast from the past!
PostCards
Stay connected! Send animated greetings to all your online buds.

STRIPS, SPECIALS, OR BESTSELLING BOOKS . . . GARFIELD'S ON EVERYONE'S MENU.

Don't miss even one episode in the Tubby Tabby's hilarious series!

- GARFIELD AT LARGE ....(#1) 978-0-345-44382-3
- GARFIELD GAINS WEIGHT ....(#2) 978-0-345-44975-7
- GARFIELD BIGGER THAN LIFE ....(#3) 978-0-345-45027-2
- GARFIELD WEIGHS IN ....(#4) 978-0-345-45205-4
- GARFIELD TAKES THE CAKE ....(#5) 978-0-345-44978-8
- GARFIELD EATS HIS HEART OUT....(#6) 978-0-345-46459-0
- GARFIELD SITS AROUND THE HOUSE....(#7) 978-0-345-46463-7
- GARFIELD TIPS THE SCALES ....(#8) 978-0-345-46909-0
- GARFIELD LOSES HIS FEET....(#9) 978-0-345-46467-5
- GARFIELD MAKES IT BIG ....(#10) 978-0-345-46468-2
- GARFIELD ROLLS ON ....(#11) 978-0-345-47561-9
- GARFIELD OUT TO LUNCH....(#12) 978-0-345-47562-6
- GARFIELD FOOD FOR THOUGHT....(#13) 978-0-345-47563-3
- GARFIELD SWALLOWS HIS PRIDE....(#14) 978-0-345-91386-9
- GARFIELD WORLDWIDE ....(#15) 978-0-345-91754-6
- GARFIELD ROUNDS OUT....(#16) 978-0-345-49169-5
- GARFIELD CHEWS THE FAT....(#17) 978-0-345-49170-1

GARFIELD GOES TO WAIST ....(#18) 978-0-345-36430-2
GARFIELD HANGS OUT....(#19) 978-0-345-36835-5
GARFIELD TAKES UP SPACE ....(#20) 978-0-345-37029-7
GARFIELD SAYS A MOUTHFUL ....(#21) 978-0-345-37368-7
GARFIELD BY THE POUND....(#22) 978-0-345-37579-7
GARFIELD KEEPS HIS CHINS UP ....(#23) 978-0-345-37959-7
GARFIELD TAKES HIS LICKS....(#24) 978-0-345-38170-5
GARFIELD HITS THE BIG TIME ....(#25) 978-0-345-38332-7
GARFIELD PULLS HIS WEIGHT....(#26) 978-0-345-38666-3
GARFIELD DISHES IT OUT....(#27) 978-0-345-39287-9
GARFIELD LIFE IN THE FAT LANE ....(#28) 978-0-345-39776-8
GARFIELD TONS OF FUN....(#29) 978-0-345-40386-5
GARFIELD BIGGER AND BETTER....(#30) 978-0-345-40770-2
GARFIELD HAMS IT UP ....(#31) 978-0-345-41241-6
GARFIELD THINKS BIG....(#32) 978-0-345-41671-1
GARFIELD THROWS HIS WEIGHT AROUND ....(#33) 978-0-345-42749-6
GARFIELD LIFE TO THE FULLEST....(#34) 978-0-345-43239-1
GARFIELD FEEDS THE KITTY ....(#35) 978-0-345-43673-3
GARFIELD HOGS THE SPOTLIGHT ...(#36) 978-0-345-43922-2
GARFIELD BEEFS UP ....(#37) 978-0-345-44109-6
GARFIELD GETS COOKIN'....(#38) 978-0-345-44582-7
GARFIELD EATS CROW ....(#39) 978-0-345-45201-6
GARFIELD SURVIVAL OF THE FATTEST....(#40) 978-0-345-46458-3
GARFIELD OLDER AND WIDER....(#41) 978-0-345-46462-0
GARFIELD PIGS OUT ....(#42) 978-0-345-46466-8
GARFIELD BLOTS OUT THE SUN ....(#43) 978-0-345-46615-0
GARFIELD GOES BANANAS ....(#44) 978-0-345-91346-3
GARFIELD LARGE & IN CHARGE....(#45) 978-0-345-49172-5

DVD TIE-INS

GARFIELD AS HIMSELF....978-0-345-47805-4
GARFIELD HOLIDAY CELEBRATIONS....978-0-345-47930-3
GARFIELD TRAVEL ADVENTURES 978-0-345-48087-3

AND DON'T MISS...

GARFIELD AT 25: IN DOG YEARS I'D BE DEAD....978-0-345-45204-7
GARFIELD'S JOKE ZONE/INSULTS....978-0-345-46263-3
GARFIELD FAT CAT 3-PACK/ VOL. 1 978-0-345-46455-2
GARFIELD FAT CAT 3-PACK/ VOL. 2 978-0-345-46465-1
GARFIELD FAT CAT 3-PACK/ VOL. 3 978-0-345-48088-0
GARFIELD FAT CAT 3-PACK/ VOL. 13 978-0-345-46460-6
SEASON'S EATINGS: A VERY MERRY GARFIELD CHRISTMAS 978-0-345-47560-2
GARFIELD'S GUIDE TO EVERYTHING 978-0-345-46461-3
ODIE UNLEASHED! 978-0-345-46464-4
GARFIELD'S BOOK OF CAT NAMES....978-0-345-48516-8
THE GARFIELD JOURNAL....978-0-345-46469-9
LIGHTS, CAMERA, HAIRBALLS!: GARFIELD AT THE MOVIES....978-0-345-49134-3

- **New larger, full-color format!**